by Jennifer S. Larson

Lerner Publications Company • Minneapolis

For Isaiah and Grace

Lerner Publications Company
A division of Lerner Publishing Group
241 First Avenue North
Minneapolis, MN 55401 U.S.A.

Website address: www.lernerbooks.com

There are two types of bison. This book focuses on American wood and plains bison.

Words in *italic* type are explained in a glossary on page 30.

Library of Congress Cataloging-in-Publication Data

Larson, Jennifer S., 1967–
    Mighty bison / by Jennifer S. Larson.
      p.   cm. — (Pull ahead books)
    ISBN-13: 978-0-8225-3485-3 (lib. bdg. : alk. paper)
    ISBN-10: 0-8225-3485-1 (lib. bdg. : alk. paper)
    1. Bison—Juvenile literature. I. Title. II. Series.
QL737.U53L37 2006
599.64'3—dc22   2005011739

Manufactured in the United States of America
1 2 3 4 5 6 — JR — 11 10 09 08 07 06

What is this huge, brown animal?

This is
a bison.

A bison is very big. It can weigh as much as a small car.

Bison have large humps on their backs.

Can you find this bison's hump?

A bison's body is covered with thick fur.

Bison even have shaggy beards.

Why do bison need fur?

Many bison live in places that get cold in the winter.

They need fur to keep warm.

Bison *shed* some of their fur in the spring. They lose fur to keep cool.

What does this big animal eat?

It eats lots of grasses and
other plants.

Bison can live in forests, meadows, and open spaces called *plains*.

Bison have to *migrate* to find enough to eat.

They have to move from place to place.

Does a bison migrate all by itself?

No. Bison migrate in groups called *herds*.

How many bison do you see in this herd?

Herd members help to protect each other from *predators*.

Predators are animals that hunt and eat other animals.

Wolves, bears, and humans are predators of bison.

How do bison stay away
from predators?

Bison often run from predators.

Bison can run much faster than you can!

Bison use
their sharp
horns to
protect
themselves.
Watch out!

Male bison are called *bulls*.
They are bigger than females.

Female bison are called *cows*.

Female bison have babies
called *calves*.

Calves have red fur when they
are born.

Why doesn't this calf have horns and a hump?

The calf is too young. It will grow
horns and a hump as it gets older.

Young calves run and play. These calves run and play together.

Have you ever seen a bison?

Most bison live in large parks with lots of open spaces.

You can visit bison at these parks.

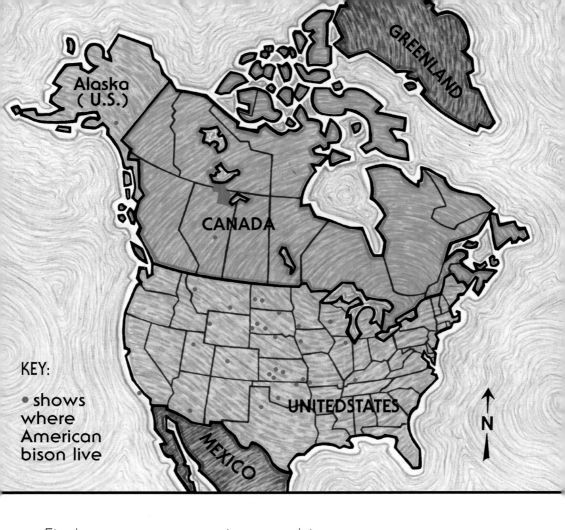

KEY:

• shows where American bison live

Alaska (U.S.)

GREENLAND

CANADA

UNITED STATES

MEXICO

N

Find your state or province on this map.
Do bison live near you?

Parts of a Bison's Body

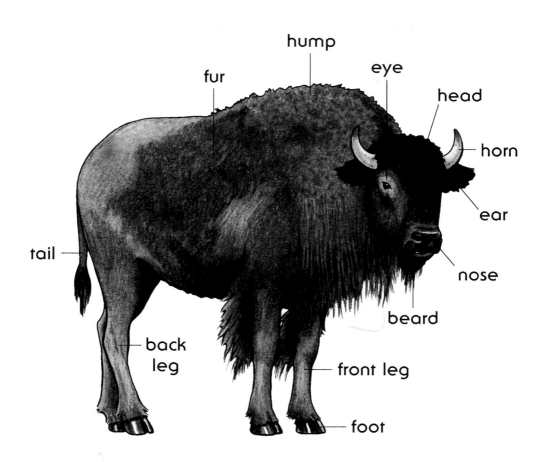

hump

fur

eye

head

horn

ear

nose

beard

tail

back leg

front leg

foot

Glossary

bulls: male bison

calves: baby bison

cows: female bison

herds: groups of bison

migrate: to move from place to place

plains: open spaces where bison live

predators: animals that hunt and eat other animals

shed: to lose fur

Further Reading and Websites

Medley, Steven P. *Antelope, Bison, Cougar: A National Park Wildlife Alphabet Book.* Yosemite National Park, CA: Yosemite Association, 2001.

Wallace, Marianne D. *America's Prairies and Grasslands: Guide to Plants and Animals.* Golden, CO: Fulcrum Publishing, 2001.

http://www.sandiegozoo.org/animalbytes/t-cattle.html

Index

Photo Acknowledgments

The photographs in this book appear courtesy of: © Beth Davidow/Visuals Unlimited, cover; © James P. Rowan, pp. 3, 7, 31; PhotoDisc Royalty Free by Getty Images, pp. 4, 9, 14, 16; © Gunter Marx Photography/CORBIS, p. 5; © Tom and Pat Leeson, pp. 6, 19, 21, 24; U.S. Fish and Wildlife Service, pp. 8, 10, 13, 22, 23, 27; Red Rock Lakes Wildlife Refuge, p. 11; © Russ Finley, p. 12; © Jack Ballard/ Visuals Unlimited, pp. 15, 20, 26; © Theo Allofs/Visuals Unlimited, p. 17; © Layne Kennedy/CORBIS, p. 18; © age fotostock/SuperStock, p. 25.